A Strategic
Global Mission

By Joel Kilpatrick

A Strategic Global Mission

The Dave and Mary Jo Williams Charitable Missions Ministry

How You Can Have A Role in God's Plan for...

- *Reaching Children*

- *Training Pastors*

- *Accelerating Global Missions World-Wide*

By Joel Kilpatrick

A Strategic Global Mission

Copyright ©2002 by Dave & Mary Jo Williams
Charitable Mission Ministry

ISBN   0-938020-57-9

First Printing 2002

Cover Design: Gerard R. Jones

Published by

Printed in the United States of America

Table of Contents

This is a familiar story for far too many of the children that we minister to.

Marietta's Amazing Story

The beautiful little Hispanic girl woke up and somehow knew she had slept in far too late. She put her bare feet on the cold floor and headed to the bathroom. She thought it was strange that it was so quiet.

No One Was There!

Marietta saw the door of her mother's bedroom opened slightly and cautiously peeked in. She avoided that room like the plague because of the men that were always in and out. She was afraid of them and hated the way they looked at her. Her heart began to pound as she pushed the door open a little more so she could look in. No one was there.

Quickly, Marietta looked back into the little room she shared with her brother and sister - they were still sleeping. She tiptoed into the kitchenette area to see what might be there to eat.

None of them would make it to school that day either. It seemed like they were out of school more than they were in anymore.

Where Is Mom?

She wondered where her mom was. She hoped she wouldn't be gone long, like she had been at different times before.

Snow was lightly falling over the city. Soon it would be Christmas! Not that Marietta had ever really gotten much for Christmas - it was just that she dreamed about the magic of it all and what she would like Santa to bring her.

Maybe she hadn't been good enough this year to get anything from him, that's what her mother had always told her, but she had really tried harder this year than ever to be good.

Her brother and sister finally woke up and joined her to watch television for a while. They brought their blankets with them to wrap up in while they shoveled down some cold cereal.

Complete Darkness

It was completely dark at 5:30 p.m., and their mother had not come home yet. They scrounged around the apartment for something to eat and fell asleep watching the TV. This scenario lasted for days.

A Knock at the Door

Almost a week had gone by when someone knocked at the door. None of the children wanted to answer it. They weren't tall enough to look out the tiny peephole. They knew if it was their mother, she had a key to get in.

They were afraid it might be one of the men that always came around. They began moving very quietly to their back bedroom.

A Man's Voice

They heard a man's voice call out for their mother. The children spoke very little English and didn't understand the term "Protective Services." They remained quiet until the man went away. Later that day came another knock at the door. They heard several voices and a woman's voice that said, "Police, open up."

Three Hungry, Cold, and Frightened Children

When the police broke the door down, they found three hungry, cold, and frightened children in a filthy apartment whose mother had completely abandoned them a week ago.

Can you believe it? She just walked out on them!

Marietta must have thought she had been very bad to have a Christmas like the one she had that year.

Friend, this is why we do what we do at Christmas and all the rest of the year for these kids.

This is a familiar story for far too many of the children that we minister to. I could fill pages with the names of children who have been abandoned by their parents. Dad and mom might be in jail, out on the streets, or dead because of the lifestyle they lead. Grandmothers, aunts, and the social system pick up the slack.

Marietta's New Life

Marietta now lives with her grandmother along with her brother and sister and attends Power Company every single Saturday. She sings in the choir and is beginning to work her way into being a helper on her bus.

In the time since her mother left, she has learned to speak English very well and has done wonderfully in school.

Her grandmother wants her and her siblings to continue being involved in Power Company because she knows that it is making a major difference in their lives.

For Marietta, the story of her life is continuing to get better. For so many others, they are still living the nightmare that Marietta used to live.

Please, help me bring a little love and joy into their lives by giving the very best financial gift you can. Fifteen bucks will make Christmas for a child; thirty dollars will bless two children.

Where can you produce so much joy and give the gift of Jesus' amazing grace at the same time for only $15 per child?

Thank you for your compassionate generosity. Charles Swindoll said, "You are never more like God than when you are giving."

Rescuing a generation,

John W. Gunn
Executive Director, The Power Company
Pontiac, Michigan

When we saw the fruit of our investment, we began to give annual scholarships and grants in order to multiply the "harvest."

A Word From Dave Williams, President of Strategic Global Mission

When Mary Jo and I gave our first scholarship in 1987 to a poor African student who was studying for the ministry, we had no idea of the impact it would make.

The young preacher went out and literally changed the face of entire cities in South Africa for Christ! He simply preached the Gospel of Jesus Christ with focus and childlike faith. The result was hundreds of lives were transformed. Violence was thwarted, and churches of Jesus Christ were built.

When we saw the fruit of our investment, we began to give annual scholarships and grants in order to multiply the "harvest." We never dreamed that our first scholarship grant would evolve into a worldwide charitable ministry that God would use to accelerate the Gospel of Jesus Christ globally.

Now, you too can have a part in this world-wide ministry. You can help provide grants and scholarships to men and women who will commit their lives to establishing churches and reaching little children before the radical cults do.

In this book, Joel Kilpatrick will take you to different parts of the world and show you the many ways Strategic Global Mission has made a difference in countless lives.

Sit back, relax, and read about the grace of God and His love for hurting humanity. Pray about providing a scholarship for some young person who will be used of God to affect his or her generation. Pray about providing a grant through SGM to an inner-city ministry which targets "at-risk" children.

Thank you for all your love and support.

Dave Williams

Lansing, Michigan

Introduction

Read This First

How would you feel if someone knocked on your door tomorrow holding a big check — for $1 million?

Would you jump up and down?

Cheer?

Cry?

Thank God?

Who *wouldn't* want that kind of life-changing surprise? And yet, there is a way in which each one of us should be jumping, cheering, and thanking God for something equally valuable.

We may not have a million dollars ...

... but each of us has a million-dollar opportunity!

Each of us has been born in the most exciting, rewarding time on planet earth — a time when the Great Commission is potentially just a few years, months, or even days from being fulfilled.

That's an opportunity of a lifetime!

This book is going to show you how *you* can help fulfill the Great Commission. *You* can cause the Gospel to go forward in effectiveness and power. *You* can help lost people find Jesus.

No, it's not a handbook on evangelism or a teaching on the gifts of the Holy Spirit. It's not a how-to book on inviting your neighbor to church. Those things are all good — but that's not what this is about.

This is a faith-building, vision-casting series of stories about people who decided they could do something to bring light to the world.

More than that, it's an invitation for you to help them! It's a chance to hold up the arms of these people like Aaron held up Moses' arms when the children of Israel fought against the enemy. As long as Moses' arms were upraised, they won; but when his arms were at his side, they began to lose.

So it is with global missions today. We have the chance to be Aarons — someone called to *give* to those who go. Or perhaps you want to be a Moses and God is calling you to go and do something with your own hands. This book may inspire you to leave where you're working and living and join the Christians right in the trenches in your city or even another country.

In either case, now is the time for all of us to accelerate our support of the mission of Jesus Christ. He is coming soon! He could come when we are sitting in church one Sunday morning or while we are on vacation in the Bahamas. He might come while we sleep or while we're talking with someone on the phone.

Whenever He comes, let's be prepared to say we did our all to make Him known to as many people as possible — people who will become our brothers and sisters in Heaven for eternity!

The focus of this book is on a foundation-type ministry called Strategic Global Mission (SGM), established by Dave and Mary Jo Williams. Dave is pastor of Mount Hope Church in Lansing, Michigan, and I am excited to share with you how God has used SGM to touch literally thousands across the globe. You will learn more about it in the coming pages through the lives of real people who have been forever changed by the ministries made possible through SGM.

Come with me now as we meet the people and look into the tender eyes of the men and women, boys and girls who came to Christ as the result of the gifts of dedicated people who helped send the Gospel around the world.

Joel Kilpatrick
Los Angeles, California

Join us as we take a look into the lives of those who are being ministered to through Strategic Global Mission.

The Hole In The Doughnut

You should drive through Oakland County, Michigan, sometime. It's one of the two or three wealthiest counties in America. Its suburbs boast some of the smartest school children in the country, and homes so big and opulent they make your eyes water. Lush lawns surround mansions with colonnades and columns, ten bedrooms, designer kitchens, and five-car garages.

But that's not all there is to Oakland County. Right in the middle, like the hole in a doughnut, is a town called Pontiac, home of the automobile of the same name. But Pontiac is different than the wealth that surrounds it. Students there score lower than almost anywhere else in the state, and many can barely read by the fifth grade. Crime is not just frequent — it's a way of life. It is so filthy and poverty stricken that even the trees in the parks seem more dead than alive.

Children like Jim live in Pontiac. Jim was six years old when something tragic happened to change his life. As he played in the back yard of his home, a man was chasing another man and they were firing guns at each other. The man being chased ran out of bullets and, trying to escape, jumped the fence into Jim's yard. The man chasing him jumped the fence too, looked the first man in the face, and pumped the contents of a nine-millimeter gun into him. The man slumped over dead, just feet away from Jim. Then the shooter looked at Jim, deciding whether to kill him too, but put the gun at his side and ran away.

That explosion of violence into Jim's young life traumatized him for a number of years. He became almost a non-functioning person. Jim wouldn't do schoolwork, wouldn't leave the house and fought panic attacks. If he heard a balloon pop it brought the whole scene rushing back, and he became an emotional wreck.

Hard Ground

Thankfully, Jim is on the way to recovery today, but that's the kind of stories that come out of Pontiac — a pit of poverty and violence in the middle of such riches.

It's stories like Jim's that caught the heart of John Gunn, pastor of a successful church in the Oakland County suburbs. Gunn had pastored for twenty-five years, often traveling the world on missions trips and to preach the Gospel. He had everything a pastor could want: a growing, thriving church, plenty of tithe money to support outreach and expansion; and stable, mature Christians in his congregation.

But Pastor Gunn found it hard to ignore the mission field only a few miles away in Pontiac. The burden began to weigh on him like a backpack full of wet sand, and he began to pray that God would give his church the answer key to the city of Pontiac — something to break the grip of poverty, drug use and hopelessness.

Then a man in his congregation had an idea. He started taking his pickup truck to the inner-city and bringing kids to the church. Pastor Gunn liked that idea so much he loaned him the church van. The man filled that up so they bought a bus; he filled that up too. A vision was taking shape, and it became clear to Pastor Gunn that children would be the key to reaching Pontiac.

You see, Pontiac is such a hard place — starting a real, lasting work is next to impossible. Many fly-by-night churches blow through promising great things, then suddenly disappear. But long-lasting, fruitful churches are rare.

That has left many people jaded, distrustful and suspicious. If you show up at someone's door and hand them a flyer and say you'll be back next week to remind them about services, they are likely to tell you to go away and never come back — and they might even threaten to shoot you if you do.

But programs for children are different. If you knock on someone's door and invite their kids to a fun program, they feel appreciative. No one else is investing in their kids, so any help is welcome.

A Radical Change

When Pastor Gunn realized this, he knew God had given him the key to reaching the people of Pontiac. So he and the church began the Power Company Kids' Club, a fun, Bible-based interactive presentation for children. They met in the old YMCA building in downtown Pontiac, and on that first Saturday twenty-one kids showed up. Pastor Gunn was pleased. He had a plan in mind of how they would use the program to plant a church, evangelize the city, install a young pastor, and help the church succeed.

That's the way they'd always done it.

But that wasn't God's plan this time.

Pastor Gunn began to see that the traditional church-planting model wouldn't work. There were three hundred churches in Pontiac already, and still the city was as lost as ever. What they needed was a full-time evangelistic effort aimed at children and taking place, not in a sanctuary, but right where people lived — in their neighborhoods, their schools and gymnasiums.

That's when John Gunn, pastor of a well-to-do church in one of America's wealthiest suburbs, made a life-changing decision. He believed God was calling *him* to Pontiac to head up this children's ministry. He couldn't ignore the call anymore.

In 1997 Gunn left the church he'd pastored for nearly fourteen years, sold his house, bought a home in the inner-city of Pontiac and began to win souls through the Power Company Kids' Club.

A Young, Beautiful Light

He wanted to win people like eight-year-old Carissa, a beautiful young Hispanic girl who came to the Power Company for three years, never missing a meeting. She even dressed Leon, her four-year-old brother, and brought him with her. Gunn saw her embrace the Gospel with childlike faith.

And yet her household was far from godly. She was always hungry because her father spent their money on drugs. Not one time did Gunn see her father sober, and her mother had no faith to change their situation. But Carissa persisted in her young faith, taking the bus to church every Sunday. She was a little light in a dark place.

One day the Gunns took her home on Saturday afternoon after a Power Company meeting, and Carissa went into the yard to play. It wasn't an hour after they dropped her off that gun violence broke out in the street, and a stray bullet struck her in the back of the head, killing her.

That little light had been snuffed out.

The shooter was never found. Later, Pastor Gunn preached Carissa's funeral to a packed house and had to threaten to kick her father out of the meeting because he'd shown up drunk and high on crack. At the viewing of the body, her father pulled a knife on a man and had to be restrained by the police.

He died three years later of cirrhosis of the liver.

Carissa's mom and Leon moved to another part of the state. As with so many inner-city stories, this one ended with a splintered family and death. But John Gunn knew that at least one member of the family had been rescued and that Carissa was waiting for him in Heaven.

*Reverend John Gunn preaches and shares
the vision for reaching inner-city children
for Jesus Christ.*

*A little Power Company girl
sings her heart out for Jesus.*

Making A Difference!

That's the kind of life-changing results that are taking place with the help of Strategic Global Mission — the foundation-type ministry started by Dave and Mary Jo Williams to advance the Gospel.

Have you ever felt like you wanted to do more to spread the Gospel to the world? That if you could only give more, or sacrifice more, or cast a bigger vision, more people would come to know Jesus?

That's how Dave and Mary Jo felt when they informally started Strategic Global Mission (SGM) in 1987. They asked themselves, "How can we be more effective than we are now in advancing the Good News? What are the areas of need on our planet?"

Of course there are thousands of places that need more money, volunteers, trained preachers and evangelists. There's probably a need right across your fence or down the block.

As Christians, we can feel the heart of God when we read about people like Carissa. We can understand the pain God feels as people slip into eternity without knowing their Savior. That is what motivated the Williams' to start SGM.

And it's what motivates people to support SGM and the ministries it helps.

The Williams' decided to dream big. *Really* big. They wanted to help the light penetrate dark places overseas and in America – in fact, right in their own back yards. So they decided to put their money into works that touched people who lived just a few miles away, and others who lived ten thousand miles away in places the Williams' might never see.

After much prayer and consideration, they gave direction to this new foundation-type ministry and are currently focusing their efforts in three main areas:

- *Number One: Making disciples of "at-risk" children.*

This means providing grants to ministries that strive to make disciples of inner-city children. Helping children learn God's laws, God's love and delivering them from Satan's lies!

Neighborhoods become safer, and entire families that were trapped in hopelessness are saved.

- *Number Two: Giving scholarships to future ministers so they can have a better shot at success.*

This means giving foreign scholarships for Bible school students in South Africa and scholarships for American pastors who want to pioneer churches.

Many young men and women who are called to the ministry are unable to attend Bible college to learn evangelism, discipleship, and church growth — all because of financial constraints. But with scholarships from SGM, that barrier is erased!

The world benefits from a well-studied, well-prepared young person who has a rich education *and* the blessing of the Holy Spirit.

Scholarships also make it possible for students to attend the Dave Williams Seminary of Practical Ministry, a distance learning institute for those already in the ministry.

The results are wonderful! Well-equipped ministers fill pulpits globally, learning genuine ministry and putting an end to church closings.

▪ *Number Three: Dave's personal ministry in seminars, missions conventions, conferences and leadership training.*

A lot of important ministry is in teaching and motivating pastors to make a strong commitment to world missions, to train them in the ways of church success, and warning them of the major reasons churches fail and pastors quit. Seminars help to inspire pastors, training them in "casting a vision" and inspiring the people God brings to their ministries.

God has taught Dave so much in more than twenty-five years as a pastor. And part of SGM's mission is to help Dave share those winning principles with other pastors who are like he was when he first entered the ministry:

• craving knowledge of how Kingdom things work,

• wanting to build a successful church,

• hungry for teaching that has a practical effect on the world.

When young pastors get hold of these Kingdom principles, churches prosper by following God's financial plan. The Gospel advances globally, churches double and triple the amount they give to missions, and the face of missions worldwide is changed! Hundreds of thousands more come to Christ, and more churches open up, grow and succeed.

SGM's three-pronged approach is to:

1. Make disciples of at-risk children.

2. Give scholarships to men and women who are called to the ministry.

3. Help Dave travel and encourage others to make greater commitments to global missions, and teach them principles of successful church-building.

Do you get excited when you read or hear about successful ministry? Does it make your day when you know that souls are won because of your contribution? Read on! There are many inspiring stories ahead!

Future ministers excited to preach the Gospel!

*But when we sow what
we have, God multiplies
it in ways that astound.*

Devil's Night No More

In a few short years, the Power Company Kids' Club — with the help of supporters like you — has become one of the most popular and trusted community programs in Pontiac's history. They are independent, not supported by Pastor Gunn's former church or a denomination, and yet they have the support of many different churches in the city.

They run a fleet of fourteen buses and sidewalk Sunday school trucks, regularly reaching 1,500 children every weekend. That's more people than in most American churches. It almost qualifies as a megachurch — but for children!

They hold school assemblies, city-wide crusades, after-school programs, and are reaching entire families through children who see hope in the message of Christ.

And here's the remarkable thing; *All but one person running the program are volunteers.* Pastor Gunn himself takes no salary, but raises his own support. A core group of a dozen volunteers work normal jobs and give the rest of their time to busing children on Saturdays, visiting them at their homes during the week, and planning and praying with other volunteers.

When you give to the Power Company, your money goes directly to the children! Talk about getting bang for your buck.

Saving Lives On Halloween

It takes dedicated volunteers, working buses, good programs, uncompromising dedication and money to reach the forgotten children of the inner-city.

But when we sow what we have, God multiplies it in ways that astound.

Several years ago, you may remember, Pontiac burst onto the nightly news when an 11-year-old boy shot a man to death on Halloween night, or "Devil's Night," as it is known in Detroit.

Devil's Night has long been a Detroit phenomenon where young people go on rampages setting fires, shooting people, and causing as much mayhem as they can. But it reached its crescendo when this young boy was booked and tried for murder — the youngest person to face murder charges at that point in America's history.

Within weeks of that sad event, the Pontiac police department called John Gunn and said, "We know you have influence in this community. Nothing else seems to be working. Please help us turn Devil's Night around. We don't want to see any more killing."

Gunn worked with the police department to put on a Harvest party during Devil's Night with hay rides, petting zoos, exotic animal displays, candy giveaways and hot air balloons. *One thousand people* came to the first party.

Five years later, at the most recent Harvest party, *six thousand* people came and enjoyed safe, family-friendly fun. General Motors and Chrysler helped sponsor it, and in the last four years there has been only one major crime incident on the streets of Pontiac on Devil's Night. The police are astonished!

That's the impact God can have through willing volunteers who take brave steps in unlikely places. Lives are saved, both physically and spiritually.

The Gospel In The Projects

Recently, a new set of low-income projects were built on the north side of Pontiac, and crime proliferated immediately. The projects' managers were totally unprepared and couldn't cope with it. They begged the police to put in a mini-station, but the police told them, "If you want a solution, ask the Power Company Kids' Club to start a Sidewalk Sunday school there."

The management called Pastor Gunn and arranged to start a sidewalk Sunday school in the new projects. Eighteen months later that project has been transformed. Crime is not the problem it was — and it didn't come through the police but through the infusion of truth into young lives.

The amazing thing is that Pastor Gunn didn't know anyone in Pontiac before starting the ministry. Anyone, that is, except the children. God has opened doors and given favor far beyond what Pastor Gunn could have done in his own power. He even sits on a community relations board headed by the mayor's office which also includes the chief of police and the superintendent of schools, working together to make the city a better place for children.

Totally Turned Around

And the stories have gotten more uplifting.

Joann was eight years old when she first came to the Power Company. Her mom was unmarried and in an illicit relationship. Joann was sent to live with an aunt in Detroit. Joann prayed every day that God would send the Power Company bus to Detroit, but of course they weren't able to go that far.

Then she came back to live with her mom in Pontiac. Her home was in the worst section of the city, but she began to bring the Gospel home with her, quoting Bible verses and telling her mom that she needed to go to church.

Her mother came under heavy conviction about her lifestyle, and a hunger for God was awakened in her. Her godmother was a devoted Christian, so Joann's mother went to church with her one Sunday and was wonderfully saved.

That was four years ago. Now Joann's mother's life has been totally turned around. She kicked out the man she was living with, received a terrific job with the county, bought a new home, drives a new car and attends church faithfully. Not long ago she started working with the Power Company as a full-time volunteer.

Being a full-time volunteer means keeping a full-time job, but giving much of the rest of the week to driving buses, visiting children and praying for the city. The time commitment is substantial, but it's worth it.

That's a wonderful example of a child carrying the light home and changing an entire family. And it happens when volunteers go into these neighborhoods and spend time with the kids one-on-one.

"High Bus"

When it comes to faithful volunteers, none is more faithful than 63-year-old Grandma Joyce. She consistently has "high bus," which means more kids are on her bus than on any of the other Power Company buses. She and her husband have been with the ministry since the Power Company started.

For years Joyce had only eight percent use of her kidneys and had to under-go frequent dialysis. Even with that serious condition she kept up her bus route, worked the program all day Saturday, *and* held a 50-hour-a-week job at a hospital.

Recently, Grandma Joyce received a kidney transplant and then came back to work. Now she needs a hip replacement and, in the meantime, continues a full schedule of visitation, even during the miserable Michigan winters, dragging her leg across the icy paths to these kids' homes. She still beats everyone else and puts 70-90 kids on a bus every week.

When you give to SGM, that's the kind of person you're supporting — someone who goes out of their way to deliver the Gospel!

The Fun Time

What happens at a Power Company meeting? Everything!

The services start with prayer, reminding the kids that each of them will spend eternity in Heaven or hell, and encouraging them to make Heaven their home. Then the room breaks into song with lots of sing-alongs, participation and humorous skits.

The music turns more worshipful, and the children are led into the presence of the Lord.

Then come the games. At every Power Company event boys and girls sit on opposite sides of the aisle and compete. Representatives come forward and answer questions about the memory verse or the previous week's lesson, to the cheers of their peers.

The adults go crazy, putting on Nickelodeon-style shows and crazy skits (one time Pastor Gunn swung above the audience on a rope wearing a gorilla outfit).

After that the tone changes and it's time for the weekly lesson. Those kids, kindergartners through fifth-graders, many who cause problems for parents and teachers through the week, sit motionless for forty minutes listening to the message. To help keep them quiet, volunteers walk back and forth looking for the quietest kids, and drop candy bars into their laps — a treasure known as the "quiet-seat prize."

The calm that comes over them is so profound that secular educators come in just to see it, because they can't believe the kids sit so politely.

At that time the kids are given a chance to say yes to Jesus, and many of them do. As they grow in the Word, even at their young age, they become little evangelists inside their homes and at school. The hope they carry with them becomes contagious.

And it continues to change Pontiac.

Bigger And Better

In their eight years of existence, the Power Company has never owned a building. They have met in five different places, all at no charge, from the YMCA to a church to a gymnasium to a rescue mission.

But now they have an opportunity to expand like never before. Up until recently they could only hold Saturday meetings because that's when the buildings were available. Recently, with the help of many church and individual contributions, they bought a 10,000-foot facility downtown which allows them to work throughout the week. They are setting up a computer lab (Pontiac schools are just now getting computers in the classrooms) and after-school tutoring programs.

Forty-three percent of fifth-graders in the city won't graduate high school. They drop out as freshmen, illiterate, and go right into drugs and crime. But the Power Company is changing that by educating them with these through-the-week programs.

Dave and Mary Jo are proud to support ministries like this through SGM, but it's only possible with the financial help of people whose hearts are touched by the plight of children in Pontiac.

Are you one of them? Has God prompted your heart to give? If so, turn to the back of the book and use the form attached to contribute to SGM.

Then keep reading. God is doing so much more!

Helping young teens smile again!

John and Michele Gunn
with Mary Jo and Dave Williams

John Gunn with The Power Company
Children's Choir

John Gunn gives a Bible lesson in the park.

All four of these young disciples were saved at The Power Company

The Power Company meeting in Pontiac, Michigan

Trouble In Lansing

There are other powerful inner-city ministries that receive SGM support. One of them is in Lansing, the capital of Michigan.

That's where Elmer and Hazel Cox spend their lives helping the children of drug-addicted or mentally deranged parents find Jesus. Yes, the Cox's pastor a church there. Mount Hope Church in the City, but they know that to save the neighborhood, they have to reach the children.

The church was in trouble when they arrived in 1996. Meeting in a little mall right next to a strip club, the church was drawing less than twenty people on Sunday, and those people didn't live in the worn-out neighborhoods nearby but drove in from the suburbs.

The Cox's started to make changes.

They held church in a house rather than next to the strip club, and when a little girl showed up alone and uninvited to a Wednesday evening Bible study, something clicked in their heads; They needed to reach the children. That's where their success would come.

Over time they built trust, rented a church building and began busing children in. Now they have a bus route through the whole inner-city and bring in a hundred kids every week!

Reaching Many

Little Chauncey lived with her aunt near the Cox's church. Her parents were divorced, and her mom was constantly strung out on drugs. Chauncey's older cousin was thirteen and, shortly after the Cox's met Chauncey, her cousin was found on the hospital steps, dead. She had overdosed on crack.

The Cox's had saved Chauncey's life but, if they had been quicker they could have saved her cousin, too.

That feeling drives the Cox's on. During summer they hold fun events in the parks, having sidewalk Sunday schools or anything to expose the kids to the Gospel.

And they are seeing success. When they first began busing kids, fist fights between the children were frequent. Now fighting is rare.

One boy who joined their church pulled out of a shoplifting gang. Doing so put his life in danger for a week or so, but he stayed with it and has left the gang life behind him.

Prayer For The Drunk

One night a drunk man came in and collapsed on the floor of the church kitchen. Some of the new kids, still rough and a bit undisciplined, saw the man in his stupor and, to Elmer and Hazel's surprise, suggested they all pray for him. They did and the man's life began to change. He came to church, sobered up, and accepted the Lord, but still had to serve some time in jail. Tragically, one morning he was found dead in his jail cell, but because of the way the kids had responded that night, we are comforted in knowing that his soul was right with God and today he is in Heaven.

Those kinds of stories are part and parcel of inner-city ministry. Alcohol runs like an evil river through the lives and homes there. Even the children have access to it. One night two boys, eight and ten years old, showed up for church drunk. The Cox's took them home and prayed with them. They never saw the ten-year-old again, but the eight-year-old became a regular and hasn't been drunk since.

The church tries to replace drugs and alcohol with food, both spiritual and physical. They serve a free lunch every weekday, and dinner on Wednesdays and Fridays. They also have a clothing room where kids can "shop" for new clothes.

One of the ways SGM has helped the Cox's is by buying them two reliable buses. Before that, they often had to cancel the program because their broken-down buses would quit running. Now they keep a full schedule with the help of buses that don't quit!

One by one, the children of Lansing are being pulled out of Satan's clutches with the help of givers like you.

Kids love to ride these "new" buses!

Reverend Elmer and Hazel Cox

*"How many want to have Jesus
as your Savior?"   "I do!"*

*For many children, the happiest
day of their week is when the
buses come to get them.*

Thousands of children have been saved from a life of violence, drugs, and gangs by reaching them for Jesus.

Praying to receive Jesus Christ!

*Hazel Cox and Diane Dalton
conduct a sidewalk Sunday
school for inner-city children.*

*Going into the neighborhoods, picking up
the children for the best day of their week.*

***Some kids would get nothing for Christmas
if not for the wonderful ministries of The
Power Company, Champion's Club, Elmer
and Hazel Cox, and others.***

Every week kids are meeting Jesus

*We love these precious children.
They are worth investing in.*

Champion's Club

Little Dewayne was a tough guy already. He had lots of energy, a mouth that wouldn't quit and an attitude to match.

But when he attended the summer program, presented by the Champion's Club, his whole demeanor changed. Not because of what they taught, necessarily, but because one of the workers, a teenage boy, took Dewayne under his wing and gave him the first positive male role model in his life.

Dewayne had only seen mean, angry men. Men who came and went when they felt like it, taking no responsibility for anyone but themselves.

But when Dewayne was shown love, his tough attitude melted away and he became affectionate, loving, playful; like a child should be.

Church In The Projects

It's all part of another awesome inner-city ministry in Lansing called the Champion's Club that has been reaching kids for eight years — right where they live.

Champion's Club is based out of Mount Hope Church and is led by Carmel Ruscheinski, a dedicated young woman who started as an intern and a few years later took leadership of the entire program.

And what a program it is! Week after week they touch the lives of children stuck in single-family households in drug-infested projects. Situations where often the only role models are the boyfriends who cycle in and out of their mothers' lives.

The Champion's Club does it by busing kids in, much like John Gunn does in Pontiac, and giving them a fun Gospel presentation as well as pizza, prizes, backpacks, games and contests.

But the backbone of Champion's Club is visitation. Every week Carmel and her four other workers visit every child on their bus route. That's 350 kids per worker. They knock on doors, sit on people's couches, and talk to parents; so when Saturday rolls around, the family is excited about sending their child to church.

Visitation makes kids feel welcome, and it helps the workers to see what kind of home life each child is coming from. If the child is violent, sullen or angry, it often means he's hurting from the awful things happening in his home.

Seven Children Left Alone

That's why visitation isn't always fun. Often Carmel arrives at a home to find that the child and family have been evicted. Boards cover the windows and, sometimes, the family's meager possessions are still inside the house. For various reasons — drug use, lack of a job, criminal history — many families in the Champion's Club target area are on the run. That may mean that the kids remain in one place for only six months or so.

Sometimes the kids will pop up on one of Carmel's other routes and the ministry continues in their young lives.

At other times, she receives calls from kids in trouble. One time a nine-year-old child called and said her parents had left her and her six siblings home alone. Carmel drove over and found them running around the house with no supervision. The refrigerator was empty, the babies unattended. Carmel brought food and watched them until 3 a.m. when the parents came home — from the casino, where they'd been gambling!

The next week the family, including all the children, was gone.

Hope After School

For every story with a sad ending, there's one with a happy ending, like Dewayne's.

But the full extent of the Champion's Club's influence won't be known until we get to Heaven. They are scattering seeds of the Gospel wherever they can, including after-school programs in several public schools, teaching the good news to as many as seventy-five kids at a time! Principals tell them that other after-school programs come and go with no emotional attachment to the kids, but the kids eagerly await Champion's Club and run to hug the workers.

During the summer, Carmel & Crew hold sidewalk Sunday schools right in the projects where parents can step out and listen without feeling conspicuous. Altogether, Champion's Club reaches as many as a thousand kids every week with a visit, a hug, a prize or a program.

And territory is being won for the Kingdom as the devil is "evicted" from these young lives!

**Dave and Mary Jo with
Pastor Carmel and two Champions**

**Dave surrounded by beauty
queens (or princesses)!**

**Dave and Mary Jo with
some of their little Champions**

**Champions enjoy a snack during
Champion's Club meeting in Lansing**

Reaching the children before the gangs and radical cults do!

Rounding up some disciples for Jesus!

**Dave and Mary Jo
with their "Champions"**

Heeding The Warning

What better way to steer America's future than by giving money to ministries that steer children into lives full of love rather than hatred, civility instead of crime, and the Gospel instead of gangs?

Most people don't realize that a large percentage of this generation of children, including many in places like downtown Lansing and Pontiac, have never heard the name of Jesus except as a curse word. They have never learned the Ten Commandments. They dwell in the inner cities and housing development projects, parts of town that most of us avoid or drive quickly through.

Many churches don't try to reach them because these kids can't "pay their way," as John Gunn, Elmer and Hazel Cox, and Carmel Ruscheinski will tell you. But the devil targets them, introducing violence, drugs, and the occult to their impressionable little lives.

Pretty soon, *everyone* pays for the failure to reach them.

If people only knew that fighting crime doesn't start when a young boy gets a gun in his hand, but years earlier when his heart is being molded. If you can get Jesus in his heart using funny skits or free meals, you've won the battle. If not, other forces will shape it, and none of us will like the outcome.

Safety First

Everyone wants safe neighborhoods and cities. But are we willing to invest in little lives before they are swept into drugs, violence, and disappointment?

Gang violence is now reaching into middle class suburbs. Maybe it's shown up in your neighborhood. Maybe your family will suffer someday at the hand of a violent, stray, unguided young person who never learned the plan of God for his life.

We can stop it before it happens! We have in our possession the most potent weapon ever known to mankind — God's Word! And we can reach these children with God's Word while they're still in the formative years, if we are willing to make a small investment in their lives.

Long-term Success

These inner-city kids are a long-term investment. No, they don't bring money into the church right away. It costs something to show God's love. The point is not tithes and offerings but souls in Heaven! Can you imagine a believer like little Carissa coming to you in Heaven and saying, "I was saved through a ministry you supported on Earth"?

Ministries like John Gunn's Power Company in Pontiac, the Cox's Mount Hope Church in the City, and Champion's Club are investing in these children. Without knowledge of the miracle-working love of Jesus Christ, they don't have a chance.

A Prophetic Warning

In the 1920s a famous preacher gave a prophetic warning to churches all over America. He said, "If we don't invest in sending missionaries to Japan now, within twenty-five years, we'll have to sacrifice many of our sons in war against Japan."

He was wrong. It wasn't twenty-five years, but only twenty years later that Japan struck Pearl Harbor. Today you can see the U.S.S. Arizona memorial built over that sunken vessel. The bodies of sons and brothers and dads are still below the surface, encased in a sunken ship that fell to Japan's bombs.

If only the church had made a small investment in sending missionaries — but it didn't. Churches were caught up in the Roaring Twenties. People were prospering. Stocks were soaring. The technology of that day — telephones — was booming, making people wealthy. American Christians, caught up in the whirlwind of the excitement, fun, and lavish living, forgot about those poor people who worshiped the Emperor instead of the true and living God.

And what a price they paid by ignoring the Great Commission!

Our Opportunity

Christians face an opportunity now that may not be repeated. God is supernaturally raising up men and women with a heart for inner-city children; people like Elmer and Hazel Cox, John Gunn, and Carmel Ruscheinski. Their ministries to at-risk children cannot support themselves. Even when they teach the children to give to God, an offering from a thousand children is likely to be less than twenty dollars.

You *can* help them! You *can* make a difference by keeping these ministries going.

Since nobody is on the payroll at SGM, any gift goes straight to putting gas in the buses that pick children up. Your gift pays the light bill for the rooms in which they gather, buys the meals, clothes, and special giveaway prizes that draw the kids' interest to the Gospel, and even pays for computers for them to learn on.

What could be closer to God's heart than children like Jim? Chauncey? Carissa? Leon? Joann? Dewayne?

Why not partner together to make *more* success stories come true in the inner-city!

Dave and his pizza buddies!

*Two of Dave and Mary Jo's
little Champions*

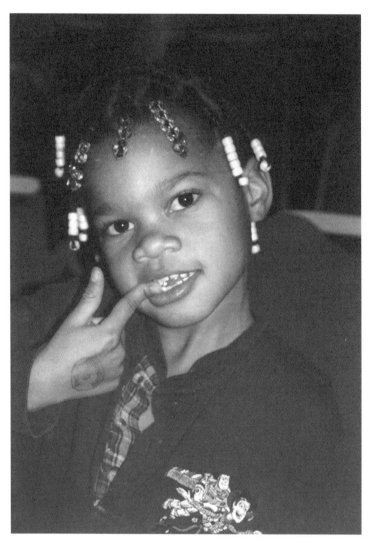

Jesus loves these children. They are precious in His sight. Just $30 a month for a year helps reach 25 children!

Gene and Phyllis Grams ministering to and training refugees from the Congo.

These students have completed leadership training and are being sent out to change their world for Jesus.

African Powerhouses!

When you lift your eyes to look at the harvest you see the children in America's cities.

As you look further, you can see people in the furthest parts of the world, places where the Gospel hasn't been effectively preached. Places torn by war and civil strife.

One of those places is South Africa, a beautiful country that has endured decades of trouble and transition. Thank God He has raised up men and women who are running like Olympic torch-runners, taking the Gospel to every village they can find!

Saints Of God

Every once in a while you meet missionary powerhouses — people who have been on the mission field for decades. They've literally sown their lives into the ground of a country not their own, and given all their energy to reach the people of a particular culture.

Gene and Phyllis Grams — beneficiaries of SGM grants — are two such powerhouses. There are hardly two more admirable people in all the world. Both were born in the Midwest and called to be missionaries at a young age. They met, married, and went to South Africa to become lifelong missionaries there.

But tragedy struck right away. Their first child, a daughter born in Africa, died two hours after birth. It was emblematic of the sacrifice they were making, and of the attack the devil would make on them for spreading the Gospel. But God is greater than the devil and He gave them three wonderful sons, one of whom is a missionary in Europe today.

Gene and Phyllis Grams embarked on an astonishing evangelism and church-planting career, spending forty-three years traveling around Africa, and helping fledgling churches. With God's help they were able to plant nearly fifty churches and build sixteen church buildings throughout South Africa.

Can you imagine! Fifty different congregations that owe their existence to you! Of course, they were God's idea, planted and nurtured by Him, but how many people are willing to be His "gardening tool?"

Gene and Phyllis are those kinds of people. The fruit of their labor grows all over South Africa.

A New Vision

Then in 1982, God gave them a wonderful new vision to start Cape College of Theology, now known as Cape Theological Seminary, in Cape Town. It was the very first multi-denominational, multiracial college in the country. It took five years to bring this vision to pass. The Lord helped them to purchase a large Catholic convent complex and, after a year of vigorous renovations, they moved in. Classes began in 1987.

Cape Theological Seminary, or CTS, started by this powerhouse couple, now churns out powerhouse pastors. Ministers who go to every part of South Africa, from the richest to the poorest, sharing the Gospel. The school sits on fifty-three acres of land on the outskirts of Cape Town, perhaps the most influential city in all South Africa.

None of this would have been possible without aid from SGM. During the ten years Gene Grams served as president, he says the most faithful and generous support came from SGM. That support has caused hundreds — if not thousands — of testimonies to flourish in that difficult area of the world.

SGM gives scholarships covering the entire cost of education, but the money is given out selectively, based upon the recommendation of the administration of the school. Students must have demonstrated a servant-heartedness, a teachable attitude, and shown that they want to draw closer to Jesus, as evidenced by prayer meeting attendance and other things.

And SGM continues to help the Grams with other needs as they arise. When they needed a vehicle, SGM provided it. When students needed scholarships to pull them out of poverty and put them on the road to leading others to Christ, SGM supporters gave and gave.

That kind of generosity has produced amazing stories like the ones I'm about to tell you — stories of hope rising from ashes.

From Stabbing To The Savior

William Tait was an aggressive young man whose temper would flare and get the best of him. Before he met the Lord he was a student at a secular university studying law. He had almost finished his degree when he got into an argument with a fellow student and stabbed him in the heart. William was arrested, expelled from the university and told that the student he stabbed had only a minimal chance of survival.

William was so overtaken with grief and remorse that he cried out to God, promising that if He saved the young man's life, William would follow Jesus and serve Him all the days of his life.

God spared the young man's life and William indeed gave His life to Christ. He was among the first group of students to enroll at CTS.

He came with a lot of questions about his future, but he was certain that God had called him to become a minister. Still, his aggression would get him into trouble, and he was easily angered by students he felt were not taking their education seriously. He knew how valuable the opportunity was.

By his third year, William had settled down and was becoming an effective minister with a bright future. But he didn't have the money to complete his BA degree in Bible and Theology. It looked like he might have to leave the school.

That's when Dave Williams visited CTS and took a liking to William, recognizing his potential for ministry. As a result of that visit, SGM gave William several scholarships, enabling him to complete his degree. Not only that, but during William's last year in school, a young lady enrolled in the college and became his wife and companion in the ministry. They now have two beautiful children.

During William's last year at CTS he began an outreach ministry in Woodstock, near the center of the city of Cape Town. Woodstock is known for its crime, drug traffic, prostitution and other social ills. Through the steadfast and faithful ministry of William and his wife, they have seen many souls saved.

For a while their congregation was without a building and had to move from one location to another, but then they were able to secure the use of a church building and build several classrooms onto it. They have completely renovated the building and it is now a beautiful meeting place for God's people. Their congregation numbers several hundred enthusiastic, dedicated, and consecrated believers.

And SGM played a part in getting William to his mission field!

William Tait and his graduating class.

Pastor Abram Moloko (left) was saved in a Gene Grams' tent meeting in 1959. Pastor Moloko's convert, Pastor Marcus Nkwe (right) was trained by our SGM missionary, Gene Grams, and now pastors a thriving church in Africa.

No matter where they go in Africa, the children flock to Phyllis. She was instrumental in bringing thousands of children together into a huge crusade during the height of the Aparthied violence in 1985 and 1986.

*Charles of the Xhosa tribe graduated
from Bible school on a Dave and
Mary Jo Williams scholarship.*

Zulu Revival

Elias was from Zulu Land, a country entirely contained within South Africa. Elias met Jesus Christ in a dramatic way and felt called of God to the ministry. But being poor, he didn't know how to get the training he needed. He knew that many cults and bondage-producing churches had been started in South Africa by those who thought they needed no Bible education.

Elias wanted to be a true man of God, presenting the truth without error.

He was an older man but started looking into Bible colleges he might attend. It was hopeless, it seemed. There was no way he could pay for the education he needed. But he prayed, "Lord, please make a way for me to be trained in your Word."

Shortly after praying that prayer, he heard about and applied for the Dave and Mary Jo Williams scholarships offered through Cape College of Theology. Faith began to rise in Elias's heart when he heard the news that he had received a scholarship. He packed his bags and headed south to Cape Town where he would make his home for the next few years.

Today Elias is the pastor of a great church in Zulu Land and is leading many tribes people to Jesus Christ. At college, he learned how to be a success and how to develop a fruitful and faithful ministry. The bitterness and anger toward those who had repressed Elias's people is now vanishing because of faith in the Savior.

Revival is coming to Zulu Land!

And the Dave and Mary Jo Williams Scholarship Fund had a part in rescuing a small country from the grips of Satan's lies.

From Generation To Generation

There are other wonderful stories.

More than forty years ago, Gene and Phyllis held an evangelistic campaign in the town of Kimberley, the renowned diamond city of South Africa. It was the only time they ministered there during their entire career in South Africa, and following the services there was a great response with people moving forward to the altar to receive Christ as Savior.

In 1988, the Grams were registering students for the new semester at CTS when they met a vivacious young lady named Sophia. She had come to the school convinced of God's call on her life to the ministry, and she was very excited to meet the Grams. She told them that her father was saved in that meeting in Kimberley long ago. He was still actively serving God and was a pillar in his church, she said, and that same faith had been passed down and embraced by Sophia.

Sophia went on to earn her B.A. degree and met a young, highly gifted man named Michael who grew up in one of the most impoverished and crime-ridden areas of Cape Town, a place ironically called Lavender Hill. Michael was saved at an early age and felt called of God to attend CTS to prepare for the ministry.

Michael and Sophia became associate pastors in a suburban church in Cape Town. Then world events conspired to change the focus of their efforts. When South Africa went through a change of government that ended the era of apartheid, the country opened its door to refugees from many other African countries. These refugees settled in the Muizenberg area, and God directed Michael and Sophia to pioneer a new church among these needy people.

Today the majority of their rapidly growing congregation is from the Congo, Zaire, Angola, Somalia and other war-torn countries. Michael and Sophia have suffered great opposition and even threats on their lives, but nothing has hindered the establishment of this new, beautiful church. They purchased a former brothel and converted it into a church building, right in the center of Muizenberg! They hold leadership meetings for people who feel called to the ministry, and some refugees plan to return to their home countries and become leaders in the churches there.

Sophia also serves as National Director of Women's Ministries for the national church.

Of course, Michael and Sophia's ministry wouldn't have been possible without scholarships from SGM. Both were very needy when they enrolled at CTS, but now God is showing that the investment in their lives was well worth it.

Growing Churches

Mike Adams and his wife, Sabrina, pastor a thriving congregation in a suburb of Cape Town. Mike didn't think he could attend CTS because of his past life of sin, but Gene encouraged him to enroll anyway.

Today Mike's congregation numbers 700 people, nearly all of them recent converts. They worship in a new building and baptize 50, 60, even 70 people at a time! Mike also has a daily radio broadcast.

Then there's Alfonso who came from extreme poverty conditions. His father was a fisherman who earned meager wages and would be out to sea for months at a time. No one in Alfonso's family was saved. On more than one occasion there seemed to be no way that Alfonso would be able to financially afford to stay in college, but that's when the SGM scholarship money would come in and rescue him from returning to the harsh world of commercial fishing.

With much testing and trial Alfonso completed his studies, took a part-time job, and pioneered a new church in a poor squatter camp, Heinz Park. He and his dedicated wife have two beautiful daughters and are seeing God build a wonderful congregation. Already they have acquired a church site and erected a steel structure.

As money becomes available, they are laying brick for a permanent building.

Pastor Alfonso in front of his new church!

Cecelia Isaacs came from a Muslim family in South Africa. She received a Dave and Mary Jo Williams Scholarship for Bible school, and today is a Christian missionary in Turkey!

**Scholarship recipient, William Tait, with his family,
pioneered a church in a crime-ridden
neighborhood of South Africa. Today the church is
reaching the hurt and broken, changing lives in
Christ's love, and growing tremendously.**

Gene and Phyllis Grams with leadership graduates at Atlantis Beacon Hill Church in South Africa. The pastor, Michael Adams was a scholarship recipient in Bible school.

Leadership graduates in Delft, South Africa. Pastor Anwar Kameldien thanks Gene and Phyllis Grams for their ministry of equipping leaders.

Hope In Many Forms

Then there's Petro, who at an early age was crippled from polio and had to use a crutch to walk. Many times people would offer to carry her books to class, but she refused saying, "I have to make my own way in life and can't depend on others to always help me." Despite her physical handicap, she was determined to fulfill God's calling on her life.

Shortly after her graduation from Cape Theological Seminary, God gave her a vision of a statue of Christ, but she didn't know where it was. In searching the encyclopedias in the library she was thrilled to discover that the statue she had seen was in a place called Sao Paulo, Brazil, and she set her heart and mind to go there as a missionary.

Petro is now in her second term at an orphanage in Brazil, despite her physical frailties. Those Brazilian children are hearing about Christ because people in the U.S. gave money to SGM, which made it possible for Petro to go into full-time ministry.

There's Colin, a former gangster, who was pronounced dead by medical officials after receiving multiple stab wounds. He found Jesus Christ in his moment of desperation, received a scholarship from SGM, graduated, and is pastor of a soul-winning church north of Cape Town, South Africa.

There's Cecelia, a single lady who graduated from CTS in 1991. She is a quiet, gentle person, but strong and determined to fulfill the will of God. This God-given strength brought her through the persecution she received from her Muslim father. Many times she was beaten for being a Christian, but she never faltered.

Cecelia has been a missionary in Turkey for eight years and has a ministry among the Muslim women of Turkey. Many times she has been threatened and cast out of her living quarters, but she never complains about having to suffer for Jesus. She is a woman of prayer and endures persecution for Christ's sake.

Saved From Execution

There's Frisko, who was miraculously saved from a northern army. He was facing execution but escaped into South Africa. He cried out to God for help and someone led him to Jesus Christ. The call to preach entered Frisko's heart when Jesus came in.

Frisko was granted an SGM scholarship. Even though he couldn't speak a word of English (he knew only French), he studied hard until he learned the language.

After four years, Frisko graduated and was granted credentials to preach. He went to Wellington and started holding revival meetings. People started coming by the literal thousands. The pastor in town, Pastor April, had to build more space in his church to fit all the people coming from the tent crusades held by Evangelist Frisko May. Because there was limited property in this south African township, the church had to be built up instead of out.

Pastor Dave dedicated the new facilities in 1996 when he and his family traveled to South Africa to present more scholarships.

Changing South Africa

Since 1987, SGM has been making stories like these possible. As a result, South Africa now has more Gospel-preaching evangelists and pastors than ever before. Cities throughout South Africa have been reached with the Good News by SGM "scholars."

South Africa is a beautiful country in turmoil. They need the true message of Jesus *now*. They have been lied to, hoodwinked, and led astray for too long.

Until recently, black people were taught by the "church" that they have no soul; that they were like animals, nothing more. As a result, many of the black people turned to Islam and other cults.

But all that is changing now. In spite of living in the murder and violence capital of the world, SGM scholars are reaching out to all races with the Good News that Jesus Christ loves, heals, saves, and sets people free!

Imported To America

There is a terrific story of a man named Clive who received an SGM scholarship many years ago. He became a pastor and a very wise leader.

Then, through a series of circumstances, Clive got to know John Gunn in Pontiac. John needed help starting an adult congregation in Pontiac — and decided that the best man for the job was Clive! Today, Clive pastors that inner-city church.

SGM money went full circle!

Still Going ...

The work in South Africa continues. Gene and Phyllis officially retired, but they are giving six months of their "retirement" every year to do SGM work in South Africa!

The reason that's so important is that South Africa is no longer issuing visas for missionaries. Gene and Phyllis achieved permanent resident status in South Africa by living there for four decades, so they have a unique and prized opportunity to keep the Gospel light shining in that beautiful nation.

In February 2001, SGM officially commissioned them to return to South Africa to mentor young pastors and strengthen the churches there. Two thousand people were on hand to officially send them back to the land and the people they love so dearly.

Today, SGM is the clearing house for the Grams' mission to South Africa. Every cent of every dollar given for their ministry goes directly to them. No administration fees are taken off the top.

You can partner with Dave and Mary Jo and other SGM supporters to speed the transformation of South Africa. These pastors and missionaries are called by God to go, and those of us who are able to give are called to support them.

With a united effort of generosity, you can help make a difference in South Africa!

Clive Williams received a scholarship to attend Bible school. Today he is pastoring a church in Pontiac, Michigan in conjunction with The Power Company.

These were some of Dave and Mary Jo's first scholars. Today they are pastors, evangelists, church-planters, and missionaries.

Hungry hearts in Africa are filled as Gene and Phyllis Grams minister the love of Jesus.

Happy faces of scholarship recipients.

Thank you SGM Partners!

Deaf People Need Jesus

Inner-city children in America, Bible college students in Africa — these are some of the needy people SGM pours resources into.

But there's another group that often goes overlooked. They may not be poor or live overseas, but they need Jesus all the same.

They Are The Deaf Population.

Deaf people, especially children, can feel trapped inside their world, isolated from everyone else. Whether at home or school or church, everything around them is geared toward people with hearing, and sometimes they get left behind.

Even churches that provide interpreters in the main service may not have the staff to help deaf children in the Sunday school room.

The deaf population can be invisible. You might see a deaf person at the grocery store or in the foyer at church and never know he or she can't hear. Being deaf presents a barrier not just to everyday living, but to receiving the Gospel.

Fa-Ho-Lo

SGM has made a special effort to reach the deaf by supporting established, effective deaf ministries. One of these is the Fa-Ho-Lo Deaf Family Camp, which began over forty-five years ago and is held each summer at a conference center in Grass Lake, Michigan.

Fa-Ho-Lo Deaf Family Camp is an awesome place! Deaf and hard-of-hearing people and their family members draw closer to one another and to God because the environment makes them feel safe and relaxed. Language barriers are erased. And the camp is open to non-Christians who can learn about the Lord, and how much He loves them.

The stories that come out of the camp each year are terrific. Recently, a group of teenagers came to camp who can be described as a rough crowd. They didn't want to be involved. They didn't want to pray or worship. They were just doing their time in the prayer service so they could get out and have fun.

But the camp's volunteers had been at work praying and interceding for them, and anointing the chairs with oil. After a couple of miserable services, something dramatic happened.

It was a Friday night, and the service was concluding early. The evangelist, somewhat frustrated, called the people forward for prayer but no one moved. Finally, one of the adults went forward for prayer saying, "I don't care if you don't want prayer — I do!"

A few of the teens came to pray for her and the Holy Spirit began to move. One by one, the youth began to pray for one another and soon they were weeping before God, repenting of their sins. Many were baptized in the Holy Spirit, and even went down under the power of the Holy Spirit. Those who were filled with the Holy Spirit began laying hands on those who were not yet filled, and those kids received!

One of the young men who was attending on a scholarship (that also allowed his family to come) had not been walking with God. He was in a gang and had become hardened. He too was touched by God and fell under the power of the Spirit and laid for hours in the presence of God. He was reclaimed for Jesus Christ that night and baptized in the Holy Spirit!

The presence of God was so strong in the room that when adults entered they were almost overwhelmed. The sound of *deaf* teens speaking in tongues filled the air, and teenagers prayed authoritatively over each other. They even prayed for the adults, and one woman was healed of a high fever.

That's the kind of fruit Dave and Mary Jo like to see!

Adults

The camp also reaches adult parents of deaf children, with the Holy Spirit ministering deeply to the needs of the people. It's common for adult campers to be at the altars for two and three hours, recommitting their lives to Jesus Christ or being refilled with the Holy Spirit. Whole families are changed and return home filled with the presence of Jesus!

But for many of these folks, camp is one of the few times they can hear the Gospel in their own "language" because they don't live near churches with a deaf ministry. Fa-Ho-Lo becomes a lifeline that fills this vital need.

The Need

Each year, Fa-Ho-Lo must raise $12,000 to keep the deaf camp operating. Campers pay for their food and rooms only. All other expenses are paid through donations. It costs a lot to pay for the recreational activities, staff, insurance, on-site medical care, travel expenses for the evangelists, honoraria for the teachers, room and food for the staff, printing, postage, handicraft supplies, teaching materials, office supplies and so on.

Like many of the ministries supported by SGM, the money goes right to the camp's purpose. The camp director, Lynn McCain, isn't paid, and the camp relies on volunteers who serve as dorm counselors, lifeguards, teachers, handcraft helpers, interpreters, office assistants and more.

Some volunteers drive twelve hours to help out!

Dave and Mary Jo decided this was a ministry they wanted to help. Many children can't attend because of the cost, even though it's only $150 for the entire week. Some families just can't afford to send their deaf kids to camp to learn about the healing love of Jesus and principles that can make them successful.

Dave and Mary Jo kicked off a campaign to send one hundred kids to camp one summer and, because of that grant many of them heard about Jesus for the first time in their lives, through sign language and presentations designed especially for them.

The results were wonderful, and SGM has been a consistent supporter ever since. Scholarships made it possible in a recent year for nearly forty kids to attend camp. Eleven of those were saved for the first time. Sixteen were baptized in the Holy Spirit. Many more made fresh commitments to live for God!

As camp director Lynn McCain says, "Seeing the power of God move upon the deaf, hearing their tongues loosed in Spirit-led prayer makes it all worthwhile."

Scholarship For A Deaf Minister

Dave and Mary Jo took their "deaf ministry" a step further when SGM helped a man whose entire ministry is about reaching deaf people. Dean Bliss, a Mount Hope member of the deaf ministry, was called to begin a church for the deaf and hearing impaired. But he needed to be trained.

He told Dave that there were more than 250,000 deaf people in Michigan, and most of them were "unchurched." Dean intended to change that!

His first step was to attend Mount Hope Bible Training Institute to be equipped to be a pastor.

Then SGM received a donation from a precious lady whose prayer was that deaf people would be reached with the Gospel of Jesus Christ. With the enthusiastic permission of the donor, SGM was able to help Dean with scholarships, enabling him to become equipped to plant a deaf church and reach the deaf people of Michigan.

Taking the Gospel to "all the world" means taking it to the invisible segments of our population, too. When deaf people learn about Jesus, it's a sign that the Gospel is reaching those who may otherwise go unnoticed.

Dean Bliss is deaf and wants to begin a church for the 250,000 deaf people in his state.

"Grandma Joyce." Kidney and hip replacement hasn't slowed this 64-year-old soul-winner down. She's reaching and making disciples of children.

Hazel Cox knows how to attract a group of children!

The Pioneer Spirit!

It's a troubling fact: Eighty percent of all new churches fail within five years.

Why?

Not because the pioneer pastors are unspiritual, but because they are *unequipped for the task*.

Dave and Mary Jo saw a better way than just watching those churches go under. They launched an all-out effort to equip those planters for the task.

What do the Williams's know about church-planting? Lots ... by experience. Of the thirteen daughter churches started by Dave's church, all are thriving today. This success comes in a day when *eight of ten* new churches close their doors within five years!

What is the missing element? Dave believes it is properly trained, properly equipped pastors with knowledge and wisdom to guide them through the many challenges, pot holes, and disappointments of church planting.

Filling The "Gospel Vacuum"

One young man, Brad Leach, had just graduated from Bible college and wanted to plant a church in Southfield, a growing multiracial suburb of Detroit. But in all of his college experience, he had only taken one practical course on church planting. That was all the college offered.

What did he need? Practical training — basic equipping. Someone to put a plow in his hand and show him how to prepare a field for harvest, how to reap that harvest, then how to plant other congregations around the city.

Brad received a scholarship from the Dave Williams School of Church Planting, a distance education program offered through SGM. The self-study program, comprised of the very best materials available anywhere in the world, takes students through a detailed, in-depth explanation of what makes church planting work.

"The School of Successful Church Planting," a complete hands-on course developed to help pastors start new churches in their communities is comparable to a master's-level study and cost thousands of dollars to develop, but SGM is able to give it free

of charge to some students so that more churches can grow and experience true revival.

Brad had the heart. He just needed the knowledge to go with it.

Brad's passion and goal is to plant a church in Southfield, where the population is divided evenly between white and black. Many churches have moved away, leaving a "Gospel vacuum." Brad wants his church to be ethnically diverse, and wants it to begin planting daughter churches within the first couple of years.

He and three other dedicated young people have started holding services in a rented building and, in a little over a year, have grown a successful church that is multiplying itself into other neighborhoods.

Young Brad and his congregation are now on the frontlines, beginning to reach a community of thousands. Brad received a scholarship from SGM supporters for the church planting course.

Types Of Scholarships

SGM gives scholarships to pioneer pastors so they can take church growth, evangelism and church planting courses at established, approved institutions like Pacific Coast Bible College in California or Western Bible College in Arizona.

These scholarships are for those specific courses — not a complete education. The purpose is to encourage students to take courses specifically about planting churches, to help turn the tide of church closings and church failures.

For example, SGM recently provided 138 scholarships specifically for pioneer pastors to take courses through Pacific Coast Bible College.

A Nightmarish Possibility

Time is running out, and Jesus is coming very soon. It seems that God is calling young people to the work of full time ministry in greater numbers than anyone can remember. But some of these young people with a call on their lives cannot afford the proper training.

When you give to SGM, *you* help train them. *You* help to keep a church from closing!

Why is this so critical? It's because church planting is the most effective way to spread the Gospel. This fact is acknowledged by every major evangelist, pastor and leader, from Billy Graham to Peter Wagner.

Followers of other religions know this, which is why they are building their temples and mosques throughout America. They are gaining major footholds. In Michigan, the religion of Islam has made great inroads because of the large Arab population around Detroit. It is said to be the biggest such population outside of the Middle East.

Dave and Mary Jo have seen up close how aggressive and effective the extremist Muslims can be in spreading their radical and false beliefs. And yet, in the spiritual vacuum that engulfs much of America, their message is getting heard often more than Christianity!

Can you imagine waking up one morning to sirens blasting through the air, only to learn that Islamic Law has been instituted in America? There are presently more mosques opening in America than there are churches. Why? Because Muslims are investing in America and Christians are lagging behind. We can stop it now... *If we are willing to make an investment in young ministers through opportunities like SGM provides.*

The Lord spoke to Dave's heart as he was praying and crying out to Him concerning the number of churches closing, and the inroads Islam has made on our inner-cities. He said that in order to reach masses of people quickly, Christians must focus heavily on training pastors, equipping and teaching them the principles of effective and successful church planting and leadership.

Dave and Mary Jo have taken that to heart and are doing all they can. Will *you* help to accomplish this great task?

Christians must focus heavily on training pastors, equipping and teaching them the principles of effective and successful church planting and leadership.

Giving

It was a wonderful night at Barnes & Noble bookstore in Lansing as Dave sat at the book-signing table and scribbled his name into the front jacket of copy after copy of his book *Radical Riches*. After two hours his hand was cramping and his eyes blurring. He wondered if his signature really looked like his own anymore!

Then a couple approached him.

"We want to thank you," they said.

"You're welcome," he replied. "I hope you enjoy the book."

"Oh, we don't mean the book," they said. "We mean the opportunity to give to your Strategic Global Mission. It's such a privilege to know we can give our money and it will go right to getting the Gospel to very needy places. We feel we're giving to what matters to God, and meeting needs that are on His heart."

What a nice surprise! It was people like them who helped make the *Radical Riches* book a success — it raised more than $100,000 for SGM through the book's sales!

That translates into over 300 scholarships and grants!

A Lasting Legacy

If there's one legacy Dave and Mary Jo want to leave to every church in America, it is how absolutely critical world missions giving is. A few years ago, Dave was invited to speak at a missions school in Springfield, Missouri. After the executive director of the foreign missions division heard Dave's message, he said, "All of our pastors need to hear this." He quickly arranged for Dave to speak in five major cities of the nation where thousands of pastors would be gathered. At that time only 23 percent of the denomination's churches were involved in world missions!

Dave traveled to the west coast, the east coast, and points in between and shared the message, "How Missions Giving Can Put Your Church on the Fast Track." In the final meeting, over *$2 million* was raised for world missions, and pastors left those meetings with a fresh commitment to reach the world for Christ.

Shortly after, when the statistics were in, they discovered that missions giving in his denomination went up by *$10 million* the following year and 50 percent of the churches were now involved in the Great Commission through missions.

One pastor invited Dave to do a missions conference at his church. He told Dave that his church was giving $63,000 to missions annually, but after hearing Dave's message, they had committed to giving $250,000 to missions — nearly a 400 percent increase in missions giving!

The Investment

What was the cost for Dave to travel to these five cities? Only $1,500. In one year, with the $2 million raised in his final meeting, and a $10 million increase in missions giving, that's a return on the investment of 800,000 percent!

Of course, Dave downplays his role in this amazing increase in missions giving, saying that so many others had a major part in motivating church leaders to participate. Yet, we know, through others' testimonies, that his role was crucial.

And now he is invited to speak all over the world on "How Missions Giving Can Put You on Fast Forward."

SGM helps Dave get to churches, mission meetings and conferences where people need to hear his message, but may not be able to pay travel expenses. Remember, nobody at SGM is paid. It is a totally volunteer enterprise, so 100 percent of the money goes into investing for the future.

God Is Opening Amazing Doors

Dave has found that as he talks about the need to give to world missions, doors have opened up for him to speak to key leaders and future leaders in the Church of Jesus Christ. He was selected recently to speak to the new ordination candidates in a particular denomination. All the executives were there, too. Right after that, he went to Minneapolis for the day to speak at the North Central University baccalaureate.

Dave wanted to impart a "Word from God" — something that would impact those graduates for all of their lives. He spoke about planting seeds for the future. Afterward, a vice president told him that in her 18 years with the college, she's never heard a more powerful baccalaureate message!

The college president invited Dave to teach a five-week course for ministers at the university the following year. What an opportunity to reach and teach future leaders the imperative of world missions!

Pastor Carmel of the Champion's Club providing coats every year to children who need them.

We love them and they love us.

Hey! What's that crinkled nose all about?

The Barnes & Noble book signing was great fun!

Meeting new friends was a blessing.

Signing case loads of books was tiring, but well worth it.

You Can Be A Partner In Accelerating The Gospel

SGM began when Dave and Mary Jo began cutting their salary to provide scholarships for foreign students who could not afford a quality education in ministry. It expanded and grew as Dave began to commit his speaking honorariums and love offerings to the ministry.

What could God do if you pledged a certain amount of your income or earnings to His work, above your regular tithe? Dave and Mary Jo have seen it make a world of difference, and they are convinced that the same opportunity is open to *anyone* who will step out in faith.

Is that the kind of opportunity that makes your eyes sparkle? Your mind whirl? Your heart beat faster?

In the year 2ooo, SGM received IRS approval to become an official 501(c)3 non-profit, tax-exempt organization.

Up to this point, SGM has been funded primarily by Dave's voluntary salary cuts and honorariums. But now that they are officially recognized as a non-profit corporation, the IRS requires that approximately 34 percent of the revenue come from public support. Otherwise, their exempt status could be revoked.

That's why it's critical that *other people give*. The vision for SGM is expanding. You have read the testimonies of lives that have been touched and changed through scholarships and grants from SGM's partners. Will you be part of it?

SGM's three-pronged focus is already producing enormous fruit for God's Kingdom. It's the safest "investment" around, and pays high dividends, spiritually speaking.

If you feel called to give to the ministries they support (remember: there are no administrative costs, so 100 percent of your gift goes to the ministries), consider becoming a monthly partner with Dave and Mary Jo through Strategic Global Mission (SGM).

You can:

1. *Change children and neighborhoods.*
2. *Install and keep effective ministers in the pulpit.*
3. *Accelerate global missions.*

Use the form in the back of this book to give your first gift … and join the team of SGM!

Will YOU help us accelerate the Gospel of Jesus Christ globally, through scholarships and grants?

We provide grants to specialty and inner-city ministries which focus on "at risk" children.

We provide scholarships to church planters in America, and ministry students in poorer countries.

Will YOU help us accelerate the Gospel of Jesus Christ globally, through scholarships and grants?

About The Author

Joel Kilpatrick is the author and free-lance writer of dozens of books, novels, and screenplays. As a magazine and newspaper journalist he has reported from five continents. Hundreds of his articles have appeared in major publications across the nation and the world. He holds an M.S. in journalism from Columbia University in New York and lives in the Los Angeles area with his wife and three children.

$300 or $30 a month can help

change the world by ...

... Reaching two "at risk" children each month.

... Providing a scholarship to an African or Asian student to learn how to become a successful pastor or evangelist.

... Providing a scholarship to help a young man or woman to learn the principles of successful church planting (establishing new churches).

GLOBAL MISSION

STRATEGIC GLOBAL MISSION   P O BOX 80825   LANSING, MI   48908-0825

Will You Be Our Partner?

With your scholarship or grant of $300 or your monthly pledge of $30, together we will accelerate the Gospel of Jesus Christ!

STRATEGIC GLOBAL MISSION   P O BOX 80825   LANSING, MI   48908-0825

Strategic Global Mission – A Dave & Mary Jo Williams Charitable Mission

Certificate of Scholarship

In appreciation for the outstanding generosity of

JOHN G. CHRISTIAN

in providing an educational scholarship for a deserving ministerial student or pioneer pastor, with the purpose of advancing world missions and strengthening the Church of Jesus Christ globally, we hereby present this certificate of appreciation.

this Seventeenth day of November in the year of our Lord, Two Thousand

Dave Williams
Dave Williams, President

Strategic Global Mission   P O Box 80825   Lansing, Michigan 48908-0825

When you give a $300 scholarship or grant, we will send you a beautiful, gold-sealed certificate with your name inscribed to express our appreciation to you for helping us to accelerate Gospel Missions globally.

Dave Williams

STRATEGIC GLOBAL MISSION   P O BOX 80825   LANSING, MI   48908-0825

Thank You Partners!
Together we are accelerating
Gospel missions world-wide.

Melanie Adkins
Jack Ailles
Dorothy Akin
Elsie Alger
Dan & Valerie Allen
Geraldine Allen
Alma Mount Hope Church
Bianca Alvarez
Michael & Katie Ambrose
Jo Anne Anderson
Joyce Anderson
Mary & Richard Anderson
Michael Andreas
Anthony & Diane Andrejczuk
James & Diane Andrews
Karen Andrews
Angela's Inc.
Mary & Richard Appelgreen
Theresa Arends
Artisan's Pride
Sara Arwood
Auburn Hills Christian Center
Daniel & Judith Avery
Daniel & Judy Babcock
William & Shirley Bailey
Michael & Melinda Baker
Cynthia Banda
Keith & Laurie Banks
Ted Barger
Kenneth & Darlene Barkema
Carol Barker
George & Diane Barker
Roberta Barnum
Brett L. V
Kenneth Beachnau
William & Carolyn Beak
David & Mary Kay Becker
Marc & Laura Belen
Bernice Bell

Bruce & Julie Bell
Sein & Yvonne Benavides
Beverly & John Bergler
Kevin & Renee Berry
Kirt & Joy Berwald
Bethany Assembly of God
Vanessa Birdsong
Belle Ann Black
Don Blakeslee
Rose Blasen
W. John & Cynthia Boester
Marc & Charlotte Booher
Chad & Lisa Boonyasith
Brian & Karrie Bosniac
Jennifer Branch
Chris & Cassie Brogan
Chris & Janice Brogan
Kathleen Brown
Michael & Carol Brown
Rodney & Marilyn Brown
Steven & Edith Brown
Robert & Sherilyn Brubacher
Brunette Roofing & Siding
Wendy Buhrmaster
Erv & Karen Burman
Paula Burton
Brijette Byrd
Alerte Cadet
Lori Callejas
Judy Calnan
Cheryl Campbell
Vickie Caputo
Erin Carney
Scott & Tonya Carpenter
Lynn Carroll
Edmund & Gail Cary
Betty Casler
Maria Castello
Center for Ministry to Muslims

If you haven't already ...
... will you join our team of Gospel Accelerators
by becoming a partner or by providing a scholarship?

STRATEGIC GLOBAL MISSION   P O BOX 80825   LANSING, MI   48908-0825

Thank You Partners!
Together we are accelerating Gospel missions world-wide.

Marilyn Chapman
Carrolyn R. Chatman
C. Childers
Kenneth & Deborah Childers
Jeffrey & Kerry Christensen
Christian Celebration Center
Christian Trinity Church
Patricia A. Clark
Vickie Clay
Amelia Compeaux
Julie Cook
Bob & Mary Anne Cooley
Matt Cooley
Jerry & Georgia Cooper
Luantoinette Corneal
Martha Corneal
Dallas Coryell
Olga Counterman
Gregory & Laura Cowles
Jane Cowles
Paul & Crystal Curtis
Daniel & Martha Jo Davis
Jerry & Lois Davis
Robert Allan Davis
Steve & Katie Davis
Diane Dawson
Richard Dawson
Ed & Mary Day
Joanna Day
Melody DeCello
Judy Dedoes
Kathy Delong
Shawn & Kelly Denny
Evelyn Devereau
Janice DeWaele
John & Geneva Dotson
Godself Dragan
David Drake
Terry Duart

Curt Dykhuizen
William Eardley IV
James & Ann Easley
Keith & Shannon Eason
Eastgate Building & Design, Inc
Brett Eckart
Neville & Theresa Edwards
Nancy Eldred
Marie C. Elieff
Julie Elsea
Embroidery For You
Brian & Annette Erickson
Evangel Church
Michael & Judith Falatko
Duane & Julie Feldpausch
Joe & Hazell Feldpausch
Larry Fickes II
First Assembly of God-Portage
Jim & Ruth Fish
Ralph Fitzner
Ralph & Ruth Fletcher
Tiffany & Damon Ford
Beverly & John Foster
Helen Foster
Thomas Fox
Erich & Erna Frank
Erwin & Patricia French
John & Denice Froiland
Tom & Jan Furman
Wilford & Patricia Gaffner
Fred & Andelia Garcia
Charles & Janna Gardner
Deanna Gardner
Jerry & Julie Garner
Linda Garrison
Hilary Garza
Jeremiah Garza
Diamalyn Gaston
Dorothy Gendreau

If you haven't already ...
... will you join our team of Gospel Accelerators
by becoming a partner or by providing a scholarship?

STRATEGIC GLOBAL MISSION   P O BOX 80825   LANSING, MI   48908-0825

Thank You Partners!
Together we are accelerating Gospel missions world-wide.

Deborah Getzen
Joanne Gilbert
Charles & Janice Gillengerten
Ed & Rhonda Gillies
Brad & Jean Gilreath
Scott & Charlene Gipson
Annette Githae
Richard & Sharon Gleason
Robert Glennon
Randy & Joan Goheen
Juan & Maria Gonzales
Good News Missionary Church
Doug & Dawn Graham
Mary Graves
Robert G. Gray
Wallace & Christina Green
Robert & Christine Gregg
Shannon Gregory
Walt & Sandy Gregory
Archie & Rose Griffith
Helen Grim
Douglas & Raelynn Gross
Harry & Bethany Gross
Mark Grove
David Grover
Richard Grover
Lillian A. Grumblatt
Stella Guevara
John & Michele
Roxanna Gutierrez
Robert & Joan Hagerman
Sally Hall
Hazen & Keri Ham
Nancy Hammock
Sheryl Hamon
Andrew & Shannon Hancock
Charlotte Hancock
Hannah Hancock
Cindy Hankins

Doris Hanley
Sue Hansens
Bob & Sue Hardaker
Jenna Harner
Kim Harris
Nancy Harris-Turk
Terry & Barbara Hart
Gary & Arlene Hawkins
Edward & Lara Hayes
Susan Hayward
Shana Hayworth
Michael & Susan Hazen
Joseph & Marianne Henika
John & Linda Henry
Nicholas Heriford
Erasmos & Maria Hernandez
Ramon & Jean Hernandez
Severo & Joyce Hernandez
Leonard Hiatt
Dean & Jean Hibbler
Peter & Mary Higbie
Leonard & Viola Hill
Ann D. Hill
Charles & Susan Hilliker
Leonard & Ida Hintz
Jeanette Hollingsworth
Kenneth & Claudette Holmberg
LuEvea Holmes
Paul Holmes
Robert & Betty Holmes
Robert & Stacy Holmes
Peter & Rebecca Holz
Shijing Hu
Dawn Hudson
Kevin & Ruth Imhoff
Rochelle & Raymond Jackson
Jolynn Jacobs
Jared Companies
Edlia Jepsen

If you haven't already ...

... will you join our team of Gospel Accelerators
by becoming a partner or by providing a scholarship?

STRATEGIC GLOBAL MISSION   P O BOX 80825   LANSING, MI   48908-0825

Thank You Partners!
Together we are accelerating
Gospel missions world-wide.

JISL Carpentry, Inc
David Johnson
Thomas & Robbyne Jones
Betty A. Kallberg
Rita O. Karn
Patricia Kay-Cloar
Douglas & Tamela Keller
Marcia Kemble
Karen Kennedy
Bradley Kenney
Bruce & Delores Kenney
Mark & Brenda Kenney
Diane Kilpatrick
Julie Kletke
Marilynn Knickerbocker
Darlene Knight
Kristin
Frederick & Arlene Kortryk
Jerry & Linda Kuepfer
Richard & Linda La Belle
Mark & Kim Laforet
Natalya Lalor
Howard & Frances Langham
Craig & Fran Lawson
Frank & Delia Ledesma
Richard & Michelle Ledesma
Robyn Ledesma
Gordon & Sharon Legrow
Diane C. Leonard
Jeremy Leonard
Teri Leonard
Harland Letts
Corey & Kristen Lewis
Karen Little
Kevin & Rosemary Little
Evonne Love
Michael Lovette
David & Patricia Lownsbery
Karen Lutz

Richard & Sandra Maas
Stanley & Melanie Malish
Salem Mangles
Dallas Marinez
Elvira Marinez
April Lyn Martin
Ann McAleer
Gary & Jennifer McAllister
R.A. & A. F. McCoy
Karen McCreery
Jerry & DeLoise McIntosh
Roy & Delores McKain
Patricia McKenna
Daniel McKenzie
Ronald & Alm McLaren
Debra McManus
Don & Elizabeth McMichael
Tina Medrano
William & Diane Miles
Millennium Builders
Bruce & Delores Miller
Peter & Bobbie Miller
Willie T Miller
Doretha Mitchell
Norm & Joyce Mitchell
Dixie Mixon
John & Deb Monroe
Gary & Mary Moon
Don & Mary Mooney
Deanne Moore
Elizabeth A Morford
Abbey Morgan
Shannon Morrish
William & Barbara Moss
Charles & Carolyn Moubray
Mount Hope Church-Corunna
Mount Hope Church-DeWitt
Mount Hope Church-Grand Blanc
Benjamin Muchiri

If you haven't already ...
... will you join our team of Gospel Accelerators
by becoming a partner or by providing a scholarship?

STRATEGIC GLOBAL MISSION   P O BOX 80825   LANSING, MI   48908-0825

Thank You Partners!
Together we are accelerating Gospel missions world-wide.

Norm & Sharon Muhling
Barbara Murchison
Pati Murray
Bill & Sandi Myers
Laura Neal
Deborah Nelson
Marilyn Nelson
New Life Christian Fellowsip
Cheryl Newby
John & Phyllis Nickels
James B. Obeilodan
Kathleen Obenour
Norm & Barb Oberlin
John & Judy O'Leary
Rita O. Ordiway
Elaine Ostling
Laura Oswalt
Rick & Vie Oswalt
Outdoor Lawn & Landscaping
David & Billie Owen
Jeffrey Page
Jennifer Parks
Randy & Karen Parlor
Christina Pasant
Tim & Jean Peltz
Dean & Lynn Perkins
Phil & Marsha Perri
Elizabeth Perry
Jenifer Pettibone
Diane Pierce
Dale Piggott
Joni Pilaske
Tom Pion
Michael & Tonia Piper
Richard & Vickie Plowman
Bret Pohlonski
Louis & Nancy Pollok
Beverley Pomeroy
Karen Powell

Roger Preuss
Norman & Lisa Prince
Terri Pulice
Dan & Lorraine Puuri
Edward & Pamela Pyret
Albert & Deborah Ramirez
Clarence & Mylene Randall
John & Linda Reagan
Cynthia Reddin
Glenn & Lynn Reed
Roberta Rennells
Bonny Rheimer
Aida S. Rhodes
Willie & Beverly Rhodes
Ruth Rich
Alice Richter
Doris & Connie Riddle
Riley's Tax Service
John Rivas
Karen Robinson
Louise Robinson
Riola Robinson
Doris & Connie Robison
Patti & Ray Roble
Frank Roop
Catherine Rossi
Armor & Geneva Royston
Loren Royston
Terese Royston
Pat & Gordon Rueckert
Carmel Ruscheinski
Ron & Pam Russell
Roseann Russell
Tom & Celeste Ryan
Mark & Vickie Sanders
Wanda Sanders
Willie & Selma Sanders
Vivian Sarbo
Gene & Mary Ann Saunders

If you haven't already ...
... will you join our team of Gospel Accelerators
by becoming a partner or by providing a scholarship?

STRATEGIC GLOBAL MISSION   P O BOX 80825   LANSING, MI   48908-0825

Thank You Partners!
Together we are accelerating Gospel missions world-wide.

Cheryl Saylor
Bill P. & Patsy Joan Schleicher
Ruth Ann Schultz
Carolyn R. Scooros
Douglas Sharp
R. Bill & Hilda Shaw
Joseph & Renee Sheerin
Joshua Sheerin
Victoria Sheerin
Max & Mary Shunk
Signature Day Spa Salon
Danielle Rae Siminski
Roger & Toni Siminski
Douglas & Diane Simmer
David & Wendy Simmons
Bryon Sitler
Kirk & Susan Slater
Kenneth & Diane Slocum
Jill Smith
Richard Smith
Sandra Smith
Steven & Elizabeth Smith
Terry & Joan Smith
Gary & Diana Smythe
Craig & Michelle Snow
Clifford & Donna Snyder
Karen Snyder
David & Michelle Sobleskey
Michael & Christy Sochay
Michelle Sorrow
Connie Souza
Jonathan Spitzley
David L. Springer
David & Kris Stairs
Mark & Tamara Stinson
Myrna Strickland
James & Teri Stroud
Kerry Stubleski
Shirley Suesz

Geri F. Swain
Connie Swaynie
Don Swaynie
Alycia Szilagye
Donald & Sheryl Szostak
Cindy M. Tabor
Fred Tabor
Frank & Yvonne Takyi
Joel & Karen Tallon
Joseph & Sharon Tallon
Joseph J. Tallon
Mary Tamez
Matthew Taylor
Travis & Jennifer Taylor
Richard & Linda Teagan
Wayne Terry
Annette Thayer
Rodney & Rebecca Thayer
The Basket Case
The Tabernacle
Lisa Thompson
Peggy Thompson
Ruth Thompson
Laurie Tierney
Roland & Pamela Tiller
Allan & Joan Timmerman
June Todd
Elizabeth Torres
Richardo Torrez
Edward & Deborah Turner
Joalice Turner
Thomas & Deborah Twichell
Gary & Patti Uptigrove
Douglas Vallad
Joel & Karen Van Andel
Bruce & Barbara VanHal
Aneesh Varghese
Mary Alicia Vasquez
Judith Velez

If you haven't already ...

... will you join our team of Gospel Accelerators
by becoming a partner or by providing a scholarship?

STRATEGIC GLOBAL MISSION   P O BOX 80825   LANSING, MI   48908-0825

Thank You Partners!

Together we are accelerating Gospel missions world-wide.

Nancy Wahl
Josephine Walker
Ronald & Leeanne Walters
Tom & Alexia Walz
Daniel & Susanne Ware
Cherie Warner
Kevin & Penelope Warner
Penny Waterman
Glenna Watters
Diane Kay Weatherby
Scott & Kimberly Wesley
Larry & Janice E. Wheeler
Lisa Wheeler
Richard White
Joel & Lois Wicks
Robert & Cynthia Wilcox
Paul & Susan Wilhite
Ronald Wilkes
Darlene Williams
David & Mary Jo Williams
David J. Williams
Dorothy Williams
Earlene Williams

Trina Williams
Doris Willoughby
Matthew Wilson
Sue Wilson
Jamie & Karen Wing
Lawrence & Linda Wing
Robert & Judy Witwer
Mary Jane Wood
Douglas & Theresa Woodard
Jack & Lorraine Woodard
Michael & Cynthia Woodard
Mary Ann Woodcock
Jason & Maria Woolford
Brenda Woolworth
Bill & Lori Wortz
Naomi Wortz
Joseph & Christine Wright
Samuel & Kristin Wright
Donald & Lee Yerrick
Gregory & Laura Young
Kenneth & Denise Young
Leslie & Chris Zenker
Sharon & Michael Zumbaugh

_____   _____

_____   _____

_____   _____

_____   _____

_____   _____

_____   _____

_____   _____

If you haven't already ...
... will you join our team of Gospel Accelerators
by becoming a partner or by providing a scholarship?

STRATEGIC GLOBAL MISSION   P O BOX 80825   LANSING, MI   48908-0825

Yes, I want to help accelerate the Gospel

Yes, Dave and Mary Jo,
I want to help accelerate the Gospel of Jesus Christ.

☐ Enclosed is my gift of $300 to provide a full scholarship for training ministers to be effective and successful in God's Kingdom.

☐ I would like to become a monthly partner with SGM with my faith pledge of $30 a month.

☐ I would like to provide a grant of $300 to help reach "at risk" children through an inner-city type children's ministry.

☐ Here's how I'll help: _____

_____

Name _____

Address _____

_____

Phone _____   E-mail: _____
    Optional   Optional

Strategic
GLOBAL MISSION

STRATEGIC GLOBAL MISSION
P O BOX 80825   LANSING, MI   48908-0825

To Thank You
For Providing A
Scholarship Or
Grant In The
Amount Of $300,
We Want To Send
You A Gift.

☐ **Dear Dave and Mary Jo,**
   I have provided a new $300 scholarship or
   grant through SGM. Here's the "Thank You"
   gift I'd like you to send me (select one):

☐ **Freddy Hayler's** *Song of Angels*
   on ☐ **CD**
      ☐ **Cassette**

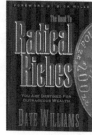

☐ **Your 400 (+) page book**
   The Road To Radical Riches

STRATEGIC GLOBAL MISSION   P O BOX 80825   LANSING, MI   48908-0825

Yes, I want to help accelerate the Gospel

Yes, Dave and Mary Jo,
I want to help accelerate the Gospel of Jesus Christ.

☐ Enclosed is my gift of $300 to provide a full scholarship for training ministers to be effective and successful in God's Kingdom.

☐ I would like to become a monthly partner with SGM with my faith pledge of $30 a month.

☐ I would like to provide a grant of $300 to help reach "at risk" children through an inner-city type children's ministry.

☐ Here's how I'll help: _____

Name _____

Address _____

_____

Phone _____ E-mail: _____
      Optional   Optional

Strategic
GLOBAL MISSION

STRATEGIC GLOBAL MISSION
P O BOX 80825 LANSING, MI 48908-0825

To Thank You For Providing A Scholarship Or Grant In The Amount Of $300, We Want To Send You A Gift.

☐ Dear Dave and Mary Jo,
I have provided a new $300 scholarship or grant through SGM. Here's the "Thank You" gift I'd like you to send me (select one):

☐ Freddy Hayler's *Song of Angels*
on: ☐ CD
☐ Cassette

☐ Your 400 (+) page book
The Road To Radical Riches

STRATEGIC GLOBAL MISSION   P O BOX 80825   LANSING, MI   48908-0825

Yes, I want to help accelerate the Gospel

Yes, Dave and Mary Jo,
I want to help accelerate the Gospel of Jesus Christ.

☐   Enclosed is my gift of $300 to provide a full scholarship for training ministers to be effective and successful in God's Kingdom.

☐   I would like to become a monthly partner with SGM with my faith pledge of $30 a month.

☐   I would like to provide a grant of $300 to help reach "at risk" children through an inner-city type children's ministry.

☐   Here's how I'll help: _____

Name _____

Address _____

_____

Phone _____   E-mail: _____
     Optional   Optional

Strategic
GLOBAL MISSION

STRATEGIC GLOBAL MISSION
P O BOX 80825   LANSING, MI   48908-0825

To Thank You For Providing A Scholarship Or Grant In The Amount Of $300, We Want To Send You A Gift.

☐ **Dear Dave and Mary Jo,**
I have provided a new $300 scholarship or grant through SGM. Here's the "Thank You" gift I'd like you to send me (select one):

☐ Freddy Hayler's *Song of Angels* on ☐ CD
☐ Cassette

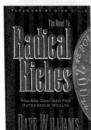

☐ Your 400 (+) page book *The Road To Radical Riches*

STRATEGIC GLOBAL MISSION   P O BOX 80825   LANSING, MI   48908-0825

Yes, I want to help accelerate the Gospel

Yes, Dave and Mary Jo,
I want to help accelerate the Gospel of Jesus Christ.

☐   Enclosed is my gift of $300 to provide a full scholarship for training ministers to be effective and successful in God's Kingdom.

☐   I would like to become a monthly partner with SGM with my faith pledge of $30 a month.

☐   I would like to provide a grant of $300 to help reach "at risk" children through an inner-city type children's ministry.

☐   Here's how I'll help: _____

Name _____

Address _____

_____

Phone _____   E-mail: _____
       Optional   Optional

STRATEGIC GLOBAL MISSION
P O BOX 80825   LANSING, MI   48908-0825

To Thank You For Providing A Scholarship Or Grant In The Amount Of $300, We Want To Send You A Gift.

☐ Dear Dave and Mary Jo,
    I have provided a new $300 scholarship or
    grant through SGM. Here's the "Thank You"
    gift I'd like you to send me (select one):

☐ Freddy Hayler's *Song of Angels*
on ☐ CD
     ☐ Cassette

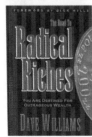

☐ Your 400 (+) page book
The Road To Radical Riches

STRATEGIC GLOBAL MISSION P O BOX 80825 LANSING, MI 48908-0825

Yes, I want to help accelerate the Gospel

Yes, Dave and Mary Jo,
I want to help accelerate the Gospel of Jesus Christ.

☐ Enclosed is my gift of $300 to provide a full scholarship for training ministers to be effective and successful in God's Kingdom.

☐ I would like to become a monthly partner with SGM with my faith pledge of $30 a month.

☐ I would like to provide a grant of $300 to help reach "at risk" children through an inner-city type children's ministry.

☐ Here's how I'll help: _____

Name _____

Address _____

_____

Phone _____ E-mail: _____
   Optional   Optional

Strategic
GLOBAL MISSION

STRATEGIC GLOBAL MISSION
P O BOX 80825 LANSING, MI 48908-0825

To Thank You For Providing A Scholarship Or Grant In The Amount Of $300, We Want To Send You A Gift.

☐ **Dear Dave and Mary Jo,**
   I have provided a new $300 scholarship or grant through SGM. Here's the "Thank You" gift I'd like you to send me (select one):

☐ Freddy Hayler's *Song of Angels*
   on ☐ CD
       ☐ Cassette

☐ Your 400 (+) page book
   The Road To Radical Riches

STRATEGIC GLOBAL MISSION   P O BOX 80825   LANSING, MI   48908-0825

Yes, I want to help accelerate the Gospel

Yes, Dave and Mary Jo,
I want to help accelerate the Gospel of Jesus Christ.

☐ Enclosed is my gift of $300 to provide a full scholarship for training ministers to be effective and successful in God's Kingdom.

☐ I would like to become a monthly partner with SGM with my faith pledge of $30 a month.

☐ I would like to provide a grant of $300 to help reach "at risk" children through an inner-city type children's ministry.

☐ Here's how I'll help: _____

Name _____

Address _____

_____

Phone _____ E-mail: _____
       Optional   Optional

Strategic
GLOBAL MISSION

STRATEGIC GLOBAL MISSION
P O BOX 80825   LANSING, MI   48908-0825

To Thank You For Providing A Scholarship Or Grant In The Amount Of $300, We Want To Send You A Gift.

☐ Dear Dave and Mary Jo,
I have provided a new $300 scholarship or grant through SGM. Here's the "Thank You" gift I'd like you to send me (select one):

☐ Freddy Hayler's *Song of Angels*
on ☐ CD
☐ Cassette

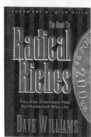

☐ Your 400 (+) page book
The Road To Radical Riches

STRATEGIC GLOBAL MISSION   P O BOX 80825   LANSING, MI   48908-0825

Yes, I want to help accelerate the Gospel

Yes, Dave and Mary Jo,
I want to help accelerate the Gospel of Jesus Christ.

☐ Enclosed is my gift of $300 to provide a full scholarship for training ministers to be effective and successful in God's Kingdom.

☐ I would like to become a monthly partner with SGM with my faith pledge of $30 a month.

☐ I would like to provide a grant of $300 to help reach "at risk" children through an inner-city type children's ministry.

☐ Here's how I'll help: _____

Name _____

Address _____

Phone _____ E-mail: _____
      Optional   Optional

Strategic
GLOBAL MISSION

STRATEGIC GLOBAL MISSION
P O BOX 80825   LANSING, MI   48908-0825

To Thank You For Providing A Scholarship Or Grant In The Amount Of $300, We Want To Send You A Gift.

☐ **Dear Dave and Mary Jo,**
   I have provided a new $300 scholarship or
   grant through SGM. Here's the "Thank You"
   gift I'd like you to send me (select one):

☐ Freddy Hayler's *Song of Angels*
on ☐ CD
☐ Cassette

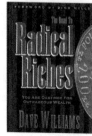

☐ Your 400 (+) page book
The Road To Radical Riches

STRATEGIC GLOBAL MISSION   P O BOX 80825   LANSING, MI   48908-0825

Yes, I want to help accelerate the Gospel

Yes, Dave and Mary Jo,
I want to help accelerate the Gospel of Jesus Christ.

☐   Enclosed is my gift of $300 to provide a full scholarship for training ministers to be effective and successful in God's Kingdom.

☐   I would like to become a monthly partner with SGM with my faith pledge of $30 a month.

☐   I would like to provide a grant of $300 to help reach "at risk" children through an inner-city type children's ministry.

☐   Here's how I'll help: _____

Name _____

Address _____

_____

Phone _____   E-mail: _____
       Optional   Optional

Strategic
GLOBAL MISSION

STRATEGIC GLOBAL MISSION
P O BOX 80825 LANSING, MI 48908-0825

To Thank You For Providing A Scholarship Or Grant In The Amount Of $300, We Want To Send You A Gift.

☐ Dear Dave and Mary Jo,
   I have provided a new $300 scholarship or
   grant through SGM. Here's the "Thank You"
   gift I'd like you to send me (select one):

☐ Freddy Hayler's *Song of Angels*
   on ☐ CD
       ☐ Cassette

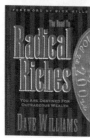

☐ Your 400 (+) page book
   The Road To Radical Riches

STRATEGIC GLOBAL MISSION   P O BOX 80825   LANSING, MI   48908-0825

Yes, I want to help accelerate the Gospel

Yes, Dave and Mary Jo,
I want to help accelerate the Gospel of Jesus Christ.

☐ Enclosed is my gift of $300 to provide a full scholarship for training ministers to be effective and successful in God's Kingdom.

☐ I would like to become a monthly partner with SGM with my faith pledge of $30 a month.

☐ I would like to provide a grant of $300 to help reach "at risk" children through an inner-city type children's ministry.

☐ Here's how I'll help: _____

Name _____

Address _____

_____

Phone _____   E-mail: _____
        Optional   Optional

STRATEGIC GLOBAL MISSION
P O BOX 80825   LANSING, MI   48908-0825

To Thank You For Providing A Scholarship Or Grant In The Amount Of $300, We Want To Send You A Gift.

☐ **Dear Dave and Mary Jo,**
I have provided a new $300 scholarship or grant through SGM. Here's the "Thank You" gift I'd like you to send me (select one):

☐ **Freddy Hayler's** *Song of Angels*
on ☐ **CD**
☐ **Cassette**

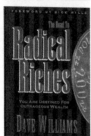

☐ **Your 400 (+) page book**
The Road To Radical Riches

STRATEGIC GLOBAL MISSION   P O BOX 80825   LANSING, MI   48908-0825

Yes, I want to help accelerate the Gospel

Yes, Dave and Mary Jo,
I want to help accelerate the Gospel of Jesus Christ.

☐ Enclosed is my gift of $300 to provide a full scholarship for training ministers to be effective and successful in God's Kingdom.

☐ I would like to become a monthly partner with SGM with my faith pledge of $30 a month.

☐ I would like to provide a grant of $300 to help reach "at risk" children through an inner-city type children's ministry.

☐ Here's how I'll help: _____
_____

Name _____

Address _____
_____

Phone _____   E-mail: _____
    Optional   Optional

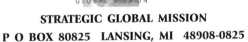

STRATEGIC GLOBAL MISSION
P O BOX 80825   LANSING, MI   48908-0825

To Thank You For Providing A Scholarship Or Grant In The Amount Of $300, We Want To Send You A Gift.

☐ Dear Dave and Mary Jo,
    I have provided a new $300 scholarship or grant through SGM. Here's the "Thank You" gift I'd like you to send me (select one):

☐ Freddy Hayler's *Song of Angels*
on ☐ CD
     ☐ Cassette

☐ Your 400 (+) page book
The Road To Radical Riches

STRATEGIC GLOBAL MISSION   P O BOX 80825   LANSING, MI   48908-0825

"Thank you for giving to the Lord ... I am a life that was changed."

Thank you SGM partners for changing lives through your scholarships and grants.

PLEASE WRITE TO US:
Dave & Mary Jo Williams
Strategic Global Mission
P O Box 80825
Lansing, MI 48908-0825
Phone: (517) 321-2780

STRATEGIC GLOBAL MISSION   P O BOX 80825   LANSING, MI   48908-0825